So.... You think you want to be a REAL ESTATE AGENT ?

TERESA ROGERS, CRS
ANN CARLSON, CRS
KENDALL E. BONNER, ESQ

Print ISBN: 978-1-54396-397-7

eBook ISBN: 978-1-54396-398-4

TABLE OF CONTENTS

INTRODUCTION

We find that many people have much misconception about the real estate industry. We see people invest time and money to obtain their real estate license only to find out it is nothing like they thought it would be. We see buyers and sellers contract with Real Estate Agents and Brokers unaware of the vast differences in Agents and Brokers, and with unrealistic expectations of what a Realtor® can and should do for them. It is our hope that this book can set some of those misconceptions straight and will help foster more realistic expectations whether you want to become a Real Estate Agent, you want to hire one, you are in an industry that supports Real Estate Professionals, or you have a loved one who is a Realtor®.

Ann and I are two independent Real Estate Agents with two totally different personalities, yet we have experienced a lot of similarities in our lives.

In our early years Ann and I were both flight attendants. As flight attendants we learned how to deal with people of all kinds in stressful situations. That proved to be good training to be a Real Estate Agent. In the early 2000's Ann and I each got our Florida real estate licenses and we met in the mid-2000's when we both moved our license to work at the same large national real estate brokerage in our area.

In 2005 and 2006 the real estate market in Florida was booming. Everything was selling, real estate was the talk of every cocktail party, and everyone wanted to get into real estate in some way.

By 2007 we had started into a free fall of real estate values that would prove to be an unprecedented real estate crash. Realtors, Brokers, Title Agents all dropped like flies in our area. Ann and I persevered through it all by sheer grit, determination, and the grace of God. It was 2010/2011 before things really started to recover in our area.

Fast forward to 2017. The economy and the real estate market had recovered and Ann and I were both doing well in the business. Ann far better than I, but we were both in the top 10 individual performers in our office of over 300+ agents. Ann and I both knew it was time to look for a new brokerage. We had some "differences of philosophy" with our brokerage at that time and we wanted to find a more "compatible" place to work at another local brokerage.

Enter Kendall. Both Kendall and her husband, Bill, are Florida licensed Attorneys. During the real estate crash they helped a lot of people restructure financially through short sales and bankruptcies. Kendall had maintained her real estate license with the brokerage Ann and I operated in. However, she left that office to purchase her own real estate franchise and brokerage firm in our area. Several people from our office decided to move to Kendall's new office and Ann and I were in that group.

We never looked back. It was a good move for both of us in our own independent businesses. And as Ann, Kendall and I collaborated to bring this book to you, I can't help wondering if there is a big director in the sky who moves people around into the right place at the right time ☺

As you read, you will see that we refer to ourselves by several different names........Real Estate Agent, Real Estate Professional, and Realtor®. They are all the same.....but yet different. You can hold a real estate license and be a Real Estate Agent and not be a Real Estate Professional or a Realtor®. When we call ourselves Real Estate Professionals it is because we have developed our real estate business, attend on-going training, and have attained credentials in our industry. We run our real estate practice as a business. Both Ann and I are Certified Residential Specialists (CRS), a designation that requires extensive training, time in the business, and minimum production levels. The designation of Realtor® requires that we adhere to a Realtor® Code of Ethics in our practice. Unfortunately, you can be a Real Estate Agent without doing it in a professional manner or operating as a Realtor®; and it's wise to remember that when you look for a licensed Real Estate Agent to help you buy or sell property.

Now come.........let us introduce you to our world.

SO...... YOU WANT TO BE A REAL ESTATE AGENT?

Well now, that would be you and half the population...... or so it seems to us. We have so many people telling us "I'm thinking about getting my real estate license". Clients, friends, family, the lady next to me on the airplane, the guy who does my pedicures. It seems like everyone wants to be a Real Estate Agent, and there are already over 2 Million real estate Agents in the US.

My question is WHY?

When I ask that question the answers are slightly different, but most can be deciphered to four main reasons....money, time, fun, people.

1. "I want to make a lot of money"
2. "I want to work when I want to work"
3. "I love to look at houses"
4. "I love helping people"

All we can say is.........you are in for a big surprise.

Don't get us wrong.......we love, love, love our profession. I've been doing it for over 18 years and expect to continue being a Realtor® until I die. But what most of you think being a Real Estate Agent is, and what it really is, are two totally different things. Kendall, Ann, and I are here to enlighten and educate potential agents, sellers, buyers, our family and our friends about what we really do. The high highs and the low lows and the crazy things that happen in this crazy business.

Today there are around 2 Million active licensed Real Estate Agents and 86,000 real estate brokerage firms in the United States.

At our office, Kendall is the Broker/Owner, and Ann and I are full-time, long-time professional Certified Residential Specialists and Realtors®. And we are here to set the record straight and give you the skinny low down on what being a "Real Estate Professional" is all about. Whether you fancy yourself as a future Realtor®, are an active Real Estate Agent now, or are a seller, a buyer, an accountant, a title agent, a lender, a lawyer, or one of our family or friends.........this book will help you understand why we are the way we are........just a little bit crazy.

And now you are going to see why.

ALL THAT MONEY

You probably think that the real estate Agent working with you to sell your house walks away with all the money shown on your closing statement as sales commission in their pocket.

We only wish. It just doesn't work that way.

A real estate agent works on a contingent basis versus a retainer basis, which means as your consultant, negotiator, and overseer of the details of the transaction, the Agent invests money and time upfront to market your home or find you a home, getting paid ONLY if, and when, they are successful.

Here is how the payment of commission works in most residential real estate transactions:

- Once a home sells, a commission is paid to the SELLER'S LISTING BROKER at the closing.

- The SELLER'S LISTING BROKER then shares a portion of that with a BUYER Co-BROKER based on a predetermined offering to Co-BROKERS through the Multiple Listing Service.

- Each BROKER then shares a portion of their commission with their AGENT involved in the transaction based on their agreed to compensation plan.

- Most often expenses to market the home are paid by the LISTING AGENT from their portion of commission, and expenses to find the property are paid by the BUYER'S AGENT.

- So, after the LISTING AGENT and the BUYER'S AGENT get their portion of the commission from their BROKER, deducts business expenses, and pays the IRS (because, of course, they want their money too) the AGENTS are left with whatever remains to pay themselves and fund expenses for their future transactions.

In effect, commission is most usually split 4 ways......two BROKERS and two AGENTS. Yes, sometimes the Agent has both the buyer and the seller, but that doesn't happen nearly as often as you probably think it does. The majority of real estate sales have one Agent and Broker on the buyer's side and one Agent and Broker on the seller's side. And if you do have "both sides", you are doing two jobs........the buyer's Agent job and the seller's Agent job.......and they have different tasks and responsibilities associated with them.

I tell new agents, assuming a usually common Broker/Agent split, that a good rule of thumb is that about 50% of your commissions will go to the combination of broker split + your business expenses + IRS taxes and you'll keep about 50% to pay yourself to feed your family. Now if you are really good at managing expenses and taxes, you may do better. But most new agents have never run their own business, so most are not experienced in the area of expenses and taxes.

A word of advice: As soon as you get your real estate license hire a good accountant to help you set up your books and plan for tax deposits, typically due on a quarterly basis. It's easy to forget about making tax deposits and the IRS doesn't look kindly on that.

Statistics say that the top 10% of Real Estate Agents make an average of $98,000 and that the average Agent makes $36,000.........and that is **commission before taxes and expenses**. Most agents work weekends and evenings and many will work 6-7 days per week, and often very long hours per day. All that money.........oh, yea........we are rolling in it.

Granted, once a Real Estate Professional has worked years to hone their skills, has gained valuable market experience, and has developed their client base, they are more effective and usually earn at a higher level. But for the first 5 years, and maybe more, it is rough and tough. It is much more like building a business than getting paid for a job. The first years are lean and, hopefully, the later years pay off.........if you last that long. Unfortunately, most do not. Statistics tell us that about 87% of Real Estate Agents quit after the first couple of years. Eighty-seven Percent??? Yep. We hope that getting a clearer look at how this business works will help improve that number.

If you have your home listed and are upset with your Real Estate Agent because your house hasn't sold, just know your Agent wants it to sell as much or more than you do. They have spent time and money on your listing and they don't make a dime until it sells AND closes. Then they must be sure that all the paperwork legally necessary is submitted to the brokerage file before the Broker will release their portion of the commission. It can be a long path the Agent takes to getting paid!

KENDALL'S KORNER.......THE BROKER VIEW

So there is a reason why they call us, "BROKE-ER"! As the Broker, you will often be broker than your agents! The business of real estate brokerages is LOW margin, HIGH volume. This means that because most splits in this business favor the top producing agents (because they have their own overhead), the broker will need a lot of business revenue passing through its doors to keep the lights on. Yet, the brokerage is also responsible for providing "VALUE" to its agents. So, what's valuable to Real Estate Professionals? That's the challenge… Real Estate Agents are a diverse group of people. Our challenge, as Broker/Owners, is to protect and serve our Agents as well as the Consumer.

But also understand this… As a real estate licensee, you are a licensed "Entrepreneur," a small business owner. You no longer have a Boss. Your Broker is NOT your boss. You are subject to IRS 1099 reporting and therefore, you are responsible for your own taxes and much of your business expenses. It's always a bit surprising to me that so many people obtain their license and don't realize this. This is one of those areas that no one really talks about, and this is one of the reasons we wanted to share our story. By the end of this book… well, you tell us… did you learn something?

EXPENSES, EXPENSES, EXPENSES

You probably thought the Broker picked up all the Agent's expenses. Well, you would be wrong.

There are a variety of brokerage structures, and it is possible that one is out there that picks up all the Agent's expenses. But, if so, the agent is likely paid a fixed amount or the commission split is very high on the Broker side. More often the Broker doesn't pick up any of the Agent's expenses or expenses to market the home. So, you might ask, "Why do Agents work for Brokers"? Easy......they have to. All commissions are paid, by law, to Brokers. **An Agent cannot receive a commission except from a Broker.** But the costs of doing business and of marketing the property are, in most cases, the responsibility of the Agent. In the case of a team, the lead Agent usually bears those costs. A Broker's costs usually come in the form of maintaining and staffing a physical office location and in the cost of training, developing and supporting their Agents.

So, when you look at the commission amount, remember that your agent is likely only receiving a portion of that for the work they do for you.

What are some expenses borne by a Real Estate Agent? National and local board dues, multiple listing services fees, telephone and auto expenses, advertising, signs, business cards, stationery, marketing materials, some staging costs, fees for business and networking organizations, training, copies, postage, mailings, internet sites, Errors and Omissions

Insurance, lockbox fees, Zillow leads ......we could go on and on. And please remember that an Agent may work weeks, months, or even **years** to make the sale. Does that sound impossible? Well, I assure you it is very possible.

That list shocks a lot of new agents who have never been independent business owners and aren't used to managing the business concept of REVENUE – EXPENSES = PROFIT BEFORE TAXES.

KENDALL'S KORNER......THE BROKER VIEW

So, while Agents have their own expenses, so does the brokerage office. We often are responsible for the brick and mortar (the physical plant), the utilities, and more! So, "the more" includes, but is not limited to, hiring and retaining highly competent and efficient staff, technology that serves the Agent and the Consumer such as websites, paperless file management systems, mobile sites, digital and print media tools to produce marketing materials and market analysis, inspiring and collaborative events and activities for Agents and Customers, in-house and outsourced training and education, file management, compliance, risk management, Attorney's fees, as well as branding and franchise fees, if applicable. And let's not forget the vanilla expenses like desk phones, internet, desks, chairs, paint, cleaners, alarms, keys, coffee, creamer, bagels, paper and ink, printer/copiers, miscellaneous office supplies, broker MLS and board fees, other association fees, signs, business cards, office marketing and advertising expenses, awards, recognition, general liability insurance, Errors and Omissions Insurance. Whew! It takes a LOT to run a business…. You have to spend money to make money!

YOU GET TO WORK WHEN YOU WANT TO WORK

Well.......kind of, sort of.......not really.

Yes, you won't have to drive downtown in rush hour traffic and be behind a desk at 8 am. You can get up at 8:00 am and start your day at 10:00 if you choose. However, the most successful agents are at work early and leave late.

Work when you want to??? No way. In fact, 24/7 burnout is one of the biggest issues in our industry and one of the main reasons for such a high attrition rate.

The first week I got into the business I sat down with a seasoned Real Estate Agent and Broker and asked her how I could become a success in the business. I was amazed when she said the first thing I needed to do was get out my calendar and mark days off and schedule my vacation. There I was ready to jump into the real estate world with both feet and she was telling me to plan a vacation. That made no sense to me at the time. Today it makes perfect sense. Not taking days off has derailed more real estate careers than probably anything else. For crying out loud, even God took a day off from His work and He says we should, too. But Real Estate Agents think the world will end if they don't answer their phone for one day. I know this because I have been one of them. It leads to burnout, folks.

KENDALL'S KORNER......THE BROKER VIEW

One of my real estate colleagues wrote in her book, "The hours are so flexible, you get to work all of them." I laughed so hard, because that statement was so true. I am also a licensed Attorney in my state and practiced law for many years before entering the real estate industry. I know that I worked "more hours" as a Real Estate Professional than I did as a lawyer. The difference maker – I fell in love with real estate and never looked back!

My best advice to Agents is that all your appointments are important, even the personal ones. You only have two commodities: time and money. You can choose to invest them or waste them. And believe it or not, TIME is the most valuable of the two. As a result, leverage is key, and to leverage your time, you must manage your activities which requires structure and intent. My belief is that conflict arises when expectations differ, so explain to your customer what you expect of them and what they can expect of you.

The same is true for the Broker and their staff as well. If you thought the Consumer was inconsiderate of your personal space and time, then you are ill-equipped to serve Real Estate Agents. If you don't properly manage expectations, agents can run your team ragged with "Got A Minute?" questions that are typically 50 minutes not 5... Typical real estate offices have to funnel calls late at night, early in the morning, on weekends, on vacations. Properly managing expectations is key to work-life balance. Thankfully, our office is not typical.

YOUNG AGENTS, OLD AGENTS

The real estate business does not discriminate. You can be old, young, inexperienced, experienced, capable, not so capable, any color, any nationality, any creed. The only thing that determines your success as a Real Estate Professional is your determination and your ability to produce results. Period. So, if you are someone who hides from responsibility for results through excuses, then forget real estate because you won't be able to hide. You either produce sales results, or you don't. Everyone is on a level playing field. There is no one else to blame.

So, if everyone is on a level playing field does that mean every agent is as good as any other?

No way!

Some agents develop and others don't. Some become excellent agents, and others won't.

As seasoned agents we've worked with them all, which perhaps is one of the hardest things you do as a Realtor®. A bad agent on the other side of a transaction is dangerous at worst and will drive you nuts at best.

Commercial Airline pilots are required to retire prior to their 65th birthday. In fact, they cannot fly even one day after they turn 65. Not so with real estate Agents. You can be 90+ years old and still sell real estate. As long as you can maintain your license no one is going to ask you to retire.

KENDALL'S KORNER.......THE BROKER VIEW

"You eat what you kill, if you don't kill, you don't eat." So it's doesn't matter if you are young, old, new, seasoned – if you want to make money in this business – YOU CAN! Many people have what we call "limited beliefs" about what they can and cannot do and why. One of my challenges as a coach and mentor in our office is to help Agents self-discover that the revenue potential in real estate is unlimited, but that requires an intentional and proactive approach, along with sacrifices, rejection, and hardships too.

FINDING THE RIGHT BROKER......A SEARCH FOR THE HOLY GRAIL

The BROKER/AGENT relationship is not unlike a parent/ child relationship. Sometimes they kick us in the pants and sometimes they support us through our tears.

Being a Broker, despite what many Agents believe, is not easy. Brokers deal with Prima Donna agents, Sloppy Agents, Part-time agents who disappear from time to time, Corporate Franchise requirements and costs, escrow disputes, unhappy buyers and sellers, unhappy agents...........we could go on and on.

They have a lot of risk and responsibility but not all the control.

When agents look for a broker they often look for:

- A good working atmosphere
- Access to on-going training and support
- A process that pays them quickly and accurately
- A fair commission split in relation to the level of support and services provided
- Being treated like a professional
- Office space and office services

Some Agents "hop" Brokers. They go with one for a while and "hop" to the next on at a whim hoping to find the perfect Broker. Others pick one and stay there, but most long-time agents have been with two or more Brokers over their career.

Ann and I feel grateful to have Kendall as our Broker. During one very busy month, Ann and I had each gone through some very trying and difficult transactions. We were both down and considerably frustrated. Talking to one another about it wasn't helping to lift us up, so we decided we needed some outside help. We called Kendall and cried for help. She scheduled a meeting with us and listened diligently and compassionately, first to me and then to Ann, telling our sad stories. And sad they were. When Kendall finally spoke she said "Ladies it usually all boils down to EXPECTATIONS". Our customers expect one thing, we expect another. "And", she said, "it is our job to set proper expectations for each transaction". We both knew she was right. She is very wise.

OH, SO YOU WANT TO BE THE BROKER

What isn't always completely understood by the public is how the Broker/Agent relationship works.

A BROKER is the entity that bears the risk and responsibility and is the entity that receives the whole commission from the seller and then distributes it to other Real Estate Professionals involved in the sale as agreed.

An AGENT "represents" the broker which means they do the work in the transaction. The Broker shares some of the commission with the Agent in exchange for their work.

Now there are all kinds of varied BROKER/AGENT agreements. In fact, no two are alike. So, it is hard for anyone, other than that specific Broker and that specific Agent, to know what the Agent is being paid for that specific sale.

To many Agents the Broker's "job" looks easy. And, oh so often, after being an Agent for a while and feeling like the Agents are the ones doing all the work while the Broker gets paid, the Agent gets the bright idea that they should become the Broker. They usually have no idea what that really entails.

Brokers have the responsibility of staffing and maintaining an office, of recruiting, training, and supporting Agents, and of all the governmental requirements relating to retaining information about the transaction.

It takes a lot of good Agents to make a Broker successful and profitable. We Agents can be Pains-in-the-Tushes…….especially the good, seasoned, talented, productive ones. We know we are good and in high demand and often we flaunt that. How Brokers keep from killing us Divas I'll never know.

KENDALL'S KORNER.......THE BROKER VIEW

So, you've been a Real Estate Agent for all of 5 seconds and now you think it would be a great idea to be a Broker. WHY??? It has always puzzled me when Agents tell me......sometimes even before they have had their first sale....... that they want to be a Broker. In my years as a Real Estate Broker, I have learned A LOT! I'm in a unique position because I am also a Florida licensed Attorney, so my background and experience have had a tremendous and invaluable impact on my ability to serve my client - THE AGENT! Yes - that's your first lesson. When you become a Broker/Owner, your customer is now the Real Estate Agent that chooses to partner with you in the success of their business. The organic mission of every real estate office is to HELP AGENTS. If you experience something different in your brokerage - RUN! Find an office that works with and serves its Agents. Better, higher skilled Agents equal a better served community. One of the many reasons Agents fail to succeed in the business and ultimately quit, is because their real estate office isn't wholly committed to improving and developing them.

TRAINING, TRAINING, TRAINING

Even after working 18 years as a Realtor® and having closed hundreds upon hundreds of transactions, I still go to training sessions once or twice a month. The business is ever changing and there is so much to know. Many new Agents think they take initial training, pass the state exam, and that's going to be it. Not even close. If you sign up to be a Real Estate Agent, you sign up for on-going training. Period. There is no way you can be an effective, knowledgeable Real Estate Agent without consistent on-going training.

Brokers vary widely in the type and amount of training they provide. Local real estate boards offer training and other real estate related companies and services offer training and mentoring as well. Some training is free, but much of it is paid by the agent.

KENDALL'S KORNER.........THE BROKER VIEW

Learn More… Earn More.

Thou shall not survive in real estate on talent alone. It takes skills to pay the bills! Marketing skills, negotiation skills, pricing skills, communication skills, just to name a few. Real estate education is continuous and monotonous.

All the greats….Michael Jordan, Tom Brady, Leonardo DiCaprio, Beyoncé…… before hitting the "stage" of their business, relentlessly master their craft and we pay top dollar to experience it.

In our office, we do our best to avoid "typical training" because we truly believe in the concept of "professional development" which is so much more than just a class. We teach concepts around mastery of skills, systems, and strategies. Because at the end of the day, doing your job at the highest level will cause more people to desire to do more business with you.

UNREALISTIC SELLERS

How do we determine the market value......the "right price".......for your home?

We use a process similar to that an appraiser uses. We search for properties similar to yours that have recently sold. We make comparisons to them, make adjustments for differences, and then come to a price or a range of price that your home will most likely sell for, based on how other properties in your neighborhood have recently sold.

Are we always right? No, we are not.

Why?

Because we can't see the future, we can only analyze the past. And you know what they say......."Past performance does not necessarily indicate future returns."

There are a lot of factors that affect what buyers will pay for your property. You can't dictate price and your Agent can't dictate price. The market dictates price.

- You over-improved your house for the neighborhood and you want to get back every dime you invested. Maybe you will, and maybe you won't. It depends on the market.

- Your neighbor got $X for his house a year ago and your house is better than his house ever was. The market will determine the value of your house, and a lot of market factors could have changed in a year.

- Your country interior design with dried flowers on every table is so adorable. You just know that everyone is going to fall in love with your house as much as you love it. Maybe they will, maybe they won't. It depends on the market.

Sellers often have unrealistic expectations of their Realtor® with regard to more than just price. They sometimes expect us to clean their house, change their light bulbs, maintain their lawn, turn their lights on and off before and after showings....... or attend every showing, which is not realistic.

As a Real Estate Professional listing your home, our responsibilities are to market your home with effective exposure to attract the highest number of potential qualified buyers; to use skill, care, and diligence in the transaction; and to manage the process from effective contract to a successful closing. We market homes, folks, we don't babysit them. Unless, of course, you have also hired us as a Property Manager for a separate fee. Then we babysit the house, but that is not part of the listing agreement.

KENDALL'S KORNER.........THE BROKER VIEW

There are several types of real estate value: Market Value, Tax Value, Appraised Value. As a seller, the value that matters to you is the one the Buyer is willing to PAY! List price and market value are not synonymous.

As a Broker, I am constantly advising our agents NOT to do work outside the scope of what their real estate license requires and allows. Outside that box is a danger zone. My advice to you, the Agent, is to stay out of the danger zone!

BUYERS CAN BE LIARS

Every real estate Agent of any experience has heard the saying "Buyers can be liars".

Why?

Because buyers lie to us.

They tell you they want one thing, but they buy another.

They tell you they are financially qualified, when they are not.

They tell you they are not working with another agent, when they are.

They tell you many, many things that are just not true.

So that is why we say "Buyers can be liars".

Tell us the truth. It will only help us help you in the long run.

OPEN HOUSES AND OTHER STUPID THINGS REAL ESTATE AGENTS DO

Every weekend you see the signs in your neighborhood...
......"Open House". That's where a Realtor® invites the public to come through their listing in the hope that one of the visitors will buy the house.

Years ago this practice made sense. Years ago you had no digital photography or virtual tours, or the internet, or Facebook, or Instagram. Years ago crime was occasional and there weren't so many bad guys and gals out there looking for any possible way to steal enough money for their next hit of drugs to keep them going.

Today, in my opinion, the practice of holding an "Open House" at a family home for anyone off the street to walk in is archaic and risky. It endangers the Agent and the family they are serving.

Think about it for a minute. Imagine you are a bad dude in need of a drug hit. You see an "Open House" sign. You see the Agent's picture on the For Sale sign. Beautiful young girl. Big, fine house. People that live there might have prescription drugs, or jewelry, or something you can steal. You go in the house. The agent welcomes you. Of course she does.......it's an "Open House". You chat with her for a minute and another potential buyer walks in. Awesome! This gives you an opportunity for free reign. You head to the master bedroom to see if there are any drugs in the medicine cabinet or jewelry in a drawer. You pass by the baby's room and see that the crib is close to the window. You unlatch the window thinking about what you might do later........

Enough??? That scenario could be written a thousand ugly ways. But still every weekend you see those "Open House" signs.

Are you kidding me?

Statistics tell us that the likelihood of actually selling a house from an Open House is less than 2%. You could easier win the lottery. Still Real Estate Agents do it. Why?

Well, it does afford the real estate Agent an opportunity to meet potential buyers or sellers. People "thinking" about buying or selling often visit open houses to evaluate the market in anticipation of a buy or sell in the future.

And, of course, because that's what agents have always done. Years ago it made sense. There were no digital photos, no internet to upload them to, no amazing virtual tours to email to potential buyers at the touch of a button. Then you held an open house because it was the only way to introduce your beautiful listing to the world.

But that was then, and this is now.

So why are we still doing such an archaic thing? And why are our seller's demanding it when there is such great risk?

Think about risk vs. reward before you do an open house, or any other marketing idea for that matter.

KENDALL'S KORNER.........THE BROKER VIEW

Wow – that was scary!

As a Broker/Owner and a citizen, safety is important to me. I care about our Agents and the folks we work for. It is true the world is changing, it feels more dangerous than ever because of the added media outlets and opportunities. I don't think it's realistic for all Agents to carry concealed weapons and such, but I do believe we all need to work smarter, wiser, and safer. Copies of photo ID should be a reasonable request, a buddy-system for checking in when working with new clients, first meetings at the office during office hours, and self-defense lessons should be taught. All of these things and more SHOULD be a normal part of our industry, but they are not…. Not for lack of trying by the Agent – it's often the consumer that rejects these changes. Perhaps after this book, more of these concepts will be accepted by the Agent and the Consumer!

WALKING IN ON ALL KINDS OF THINGS

A friend and fellow Realtor® tells a true story about a day she was showing a couple a house. She had called for the appointment to see the house and was given confirmation for the showing time she requested.......an hour slot of time from 2:00 to 3:00 pm in the afternoon. The Agent and her clients get to the house and, as is our custom even with a scheduled showing, she rings the doorbell. No one answers. She opens the lockbox with her Supra E Key lockbox program on her phone, opens the door with the key from the lockbox, and she and her clients enter the home. They look around the living room and on into the kitchen. Then down a hallway where a door is closed. She opens the door with her buyers following close behind. There on the bed is a couple in full-fledged sex. The agent quickly shuts the door and suggests they leave and come back at a better time. The couple on the bed never acknowledged them.

Oh yes, it happens.

Then there was the time I was showing a nice home in a gated community that had a bird that flew around the house. Bird poop was everywhere.......and I do mean everywhere!

Or the time when I got to the door of a scheduled showing with my buyers, rang the doorbell, and heard a very large dog barking. No one answered the door. So I called the Listing Agent and told her that I had a scheduled appointment and that I rang the doorbell and no one answered except a big dog barking wildly. "Oh, she said, "go ahead and use the lockbox. The dog is friendly". So I did. As I opened the door I see what looked to me to be a big pit-bull-type dog. My buyers really wanted to see this house so I said "Let me go in and see if he is ok". Now I ask you.......what kind of stupid is that?

Sometimes we think we're in Animal House. Cats, dogs, snakes, roaches, lizards (big ones), teenagers. You never know what you are going to encounter when you visit a house. Luckily, I don't have a keen sense of smell. That is a blessing for a Real Estate Agent.

THE REAL ESTATE SUPPORT TEAM

They say it takes a village, and in our world of real estate sales it really does. As real estate Agents we are like the quarterback of a football team. We are the center of the action, but in no way can we do it by ourselves. We have lenders, title agents, marketing companies, sign companies, transaction coordinators, handymen, and a myriad of support people that are involved in our sales.

Seasoned Real Estate Professionals have spent years searching for the best of the best support partners to insure that every transaction goes as smoothly as it possibly can. Real Estate transactions are complex and having a tried and true group of professionals working on it makes for a greater chance that the process goes smoothly and difficulties are handled with care and diligence.

KENDALL'S KORNER.........THE BROKER VIEW

There are so many players in the game of real estate. We have already mentioned several, and we should not forget the home inspector, the home warranty representative, the termite inspector, just to name a few more. There are so many companies and individuals that are intricate to a smooth and successful transaction. The real estate Agent is the conductor who is managing, connecting, and delegating to the appropriate person so that the job gets done efficiently and effectively.

WORKING WITH FRIENDS AND FAMILY.......AND I THOUGHT YOU LOVED ME

It is common knowledge that every family has its crazies and its bullies. May heaven help you if one of them wants you to help them buy or sell a home.

Everyone tries to get us to discount our sales commission, and it amazes me that our friends and family are the worst. They expect us to work extra hard for them and do it at a major discount. I wonder how they would feel if I asked them to fork over their paycheck on Friday just because I am their friend or their cousin? OK......if it's your Mom, that's different.

Always remember that if your agent can't negotiate a decent commission for their hard work, then how on earth do you think they will be able to negotiate a top sales price for your property? Makes no sense. If they easily give away their own money, trust me, yours will go even faster.

When your friend or your family member treats you unfairly it hurts even worse than when a customer off the street does. Every Real Estate Agent who has been selling for any time at all has a story of how a friend or family member hurt them to the core. Some Agents refer friends and family to another competent Agent so as not to put themselves in a position to have the transaction affect their relationship. That bad?? Oh, yeah.

KENDALL'S KORNER.......THE BROKER'S VIEW

There are three types of business.......Repeat, Referral, and New. And there are two groups of people....... the ones you know and the people you don't know. A successful real estate business requires prospecting for business. Your goal will be to build a group of people that know, like and trust you for repeat and referral business, but you will also have to seek new business from people you don't know. That is the science of the business. While a handful of people you know might call you to do business, that is not nearly enough to survive and be successful in real estate.

BUYER FEEDBACK

Sellers are so anxious to get buyer feedback. Until we get some and it's not what they hoped to hear and they get mad at their Agent for delivering it. Sellers, beware.......buyer's feedback is not what you hope it will be. In fact, it is almost irrelevant.

First, buyer's rarely give feedback that is going to be helpful to you. Why?

1. If they are not interested in the house, they are just not interested. They are concerned with their buy.......not with your sell. If it doesn't work for them, they are on to the next one and they don't think two more thoughts about your listing.

2. If they are interested in your house they won't want you to know they like it and are interested until they decide to write an offer. They fear it will give you an advantage and might hurt their negotiating position.

Sellers, if you've had 10 showings and no offers, then you have a price issue. A buyer is not going to say "Oh, gosh, you are over-priced". They will just keep looking until they find a better value. So don't expect to get showing feedback about your price. And if you do, then rest assured, it is way over-priced.

It is hard as heck for listing agents to even get buyer's Agents to provide feedback. A buyer's Agent can show countless houses in a day and they do not have the time or desire to provide feedback on all of them. Your listing Agent can write, call, beg, send a cute carrier pigeon, and still not get feedback. And when the buyer's Agent is kind enough to respond they often give very generic feedback like "They didn't like the floor plan".........even when all the buyer said was "I don't like it". When they say that, their Agent moves on to the next one. The buyer's Agent and the buyer are focused on their agenda........finding a home, not on your agenda to sell your home. Sorry, but we can't control that.

Ok, occasionally we do get some feedback that is valuable. Feedback like "The sellers really should paint and put in new flooring". Sellers usually don't like that valuable feedback. They don't want to do that or they would have done it when their Agent suggested it before listing the property. Nine out of 10 times your Agent told you what to do and you just refused to listen.

So, bottom line.......don't be so concerned about all the buyer's feedback. Buyer feedback is irrelevant. True feedback comes in the form of offers.

KENDALL'S KORNER.........THE BROKER VIEW

A buyer's feedback is limited. It's limited to their knowledge and experience, which in contrast to an experienced Real Estate Professional, is really nominal. The only buyer feedback you can trust are showings and offers! Listen to the PROFESSIONAL you hired. Either you trust the Real Estate Professional you chose to partner with, in what is often the biggest investment you have made in your life, or you don't........... And if you don't, why did you hire them in the first place? If the Agent makes a recommendation, believe that they want this transaction to succeed as much you do. They are trying to help you!

THE CRAZIES

Being a Realtor® puts you in a unique relationship with your customers. You can spend many hours traveling in a car with buyers looking at houses, you will know your customer's financial situation, their family dynamics, their work situation. For the time that you are helping them buy a house or sell their home you become almost like a member of their family. And we all know every family has its crazies.

We live in a very stressful world. People are facing issues and problems and are often over-stressed, never more than when they are full blown in the middle of moving their home........ their base of security. Few people deal properly with their stress. Some try to medicate it away, others try to drink it away, others vomit it up on those around them. And you, Dear Real Estate Agent, are in prime position to get thrown up on.

I'll give you the same advice that a long time, successful Realtor® once gave me: "Don't take it personally."

That advice can be very hard to implement, and it can take years of practice to get good at it. But you must not take your customer's words and actions personally, and you must not engage with crazies and bullies. They try to pull you into their world of chaos. Do not go there. Remain balanced, remain logical, and back away when necessary. Someone needs to be sane in the situation. You are not going to change a crazy or a bully. You can only decide how you will respond. The best way is quietly, simply, and logically. Remember that you are their Realtor®, not their doctor, psychiatrist, or whipping post.

Back away and disengage when they start being verbally and emotionally abusive. If it becomes extreme it may be necessary to fire them or work to transfer them to another agent.

All that being said, you can expect some tension in almost every sale, even when you are dealing with rational, logical, normally sane people. A real estate transaction transpires over weeks and sometimes months. It involves many, many details and numerous people, especially when there is a mortgage loan involved, which is often the case. You can't escape the tension. But when it turns from normal tension associated with the very trying time of a physical move of their home to what feels abusive and abnormal, you must learn how to detach. Your livelihood depends on it.

KENDALL'S KORNER.........THE BROKER VIEW

Residential Real Estate is an emotional business. Part of an Agent's experience in this business, is "RE-TELL" Therapy! The relationship between a consumer and their Agent is a complicated one. It often contemplates both personal and professional concerns. Not to mention that buying and selling a home is inherently stressful and the target and outlet of consumers is the Real Estate Agent and/or their Broker. We will get blamed for things outside our control, we will be accused of things that we did not do, and we will be resented by some individuals for doing our job well (i.e. the home sold quickly, so therefore we don't deserve the agreed upon compensation). [Insert eye-roll and smack to one's own forehead] PS. BEWARE...

there are a few crazy licensees out there as well. You'll know them when you meet them!

WORKING BOTH SIDES OF THE TRANSACTION

People, including real estate Agents, often believe that it is great for a real estate Agent to "get both sides" of a transaction rather than co-broking it with another multiple listing Broker. In this case both buyer and seller use one Agent.

I've never thought that was easy.

Yes, if you bring the buyer to one of your listings and it results in a sale you get paid "both sides".......but you also have a tightrope to walk. Both buyer and seller are looking to you to look out for their interests and lead them through the transaction. That is hard to do when you are leading both sides. You have to be ultra-careful to be fair and honest and impartial.

I find that when I work with both sides invariably each side believes I am working harder for the other side, even when that is not true. But perception is often stronger than reality.

If the transaction is easy and without issue, we have no problem. But many issues can arise in a transaction, and that's when it's even more challenging when you are responsible for helping both parties.

KENDALL'S KORNER.........THE BROKER VIEW

Dual Agency in our state (Florida) is illegal. A Transaction Brokerage Relationship is the most common and is the default brokerage relationship in our state. Florida law allows for Single Agency relationship, which requires fiduciary duties to the customer. Lastly, Florida allows for Non-Representation as well, which is the most basic of the agency relationships. Each state has its own real estate laws. Buyers, Sellers, and Agents – pay attention to the type of agency relationship you agree to. None of them are perfect. It's just a matter of setting, meeting, and exceeding expectations!

YOU'RE FIRED!

On Donald Trump's show The Apprentice, he prided him-self on his ability to say "You're Fired!". As a Real Estate Agent you will need to learn that skill...... in a genteel, respectful way.

When you start working with a buyer or a seller and it becomes obvious it is not a good "fit" between you and the customer, your best option is to politely bow out and "fire them". A truly difficult buyer or seller will cost you more than you will ever make from the sale. It doesn't have to mean that they are "bad" people or that you are a "bad" person.........but your chemistry doesn't connect and the personal and business philosophies don't mesh. The longer you hang on to try to make it work, the more time and money you will invest and it rarely works out well. That is a tough lesson for new agents who are so happy to get a buyer or seller to work with that they ignore the red flags. It's a good idea to have a fellow agent that you can offer to refer to people you just don't want to work with. Perhaps it will work well for them.

When you see that someone is being abusive, demeaning, overly rude, or just a plain jerk or jerkette....... remember that you can fire them. Always, always, always do so gently, gracefully, and respectfully, but don't hold on too long in hopes that the nicer and more helpful you are they will follow suit......because they won't. And you deserve better. Work with people you like and respect and that like and respect you. Your business will be better for it.

Our time is the most valuable and precious commodity we have. It is an unrenewable resource. You can steal $100 out of my purse and I can make another $100 and replace it. But if you steal an hour of my time, I can NEVER get that hour back. It is gone forever. No recovery. Yet people steal real estate Agent's time all the time. And we, very often, allow it because we are afraid to say the word NO.

KENDALL'S KORNER.........THE BROKER VIEW

I'll never forget the first time I fired an Agent – I honestly don't think they understood what I was doing at first because it is so rare for a Broker to fire a producing Agent. I have a saying, "Not all money is good money" meaning I won't sacrifice my morals, my peace of mind, and my livelihood for a dollar (or for many dollars as the case may be)! I would rather replace that income than suffer for it. If you have ever had to "fire" someone, you know that it is emotionally taxing.

So here's the lesson.... I'll remind you that you have three budgets to invest or to waste: Time, Money and Energy. If someone is causing you stress or wasting your valuable time, money and energy – stop the bleeding! The relief you will feel when the deed is done is worth so much more.

SURVIVING THE "U"

The initial vision of this book was to educate people on what being a Realtor® is really like. But as we started writing it, I realized it is also a reflection of the history of one of the most tumultuous times in the history of real estate in the United States. Ann and I were smack dab at the epicenter of it, in one of the hardest hit areas of the country, during the real estate meltdown of 2007 to 2010.

From 2007 through 2010 many real estate markets in the US experienced unprecedented drops in values. Florida was one of those markets hardest hit. Ann and I were full time, active Agents who found ourselves right in the middle of the mess. And a mess it was! We could write a whole book about how ugly, how brutal that period was for everyone involved in real estate. But, for now, let's just say it taught us a lot about survival and it taught us that what is up can come down………… and, very thankfully, can rebound back up again.

No one, least of all us, predicted how bad it could get. In the middle of it you felt like you were in a freefall and you couldn't know where or when the bottom would come. Many Real Estate Agents, Brokers, lenders, and title people got out of the business because they just couldn't make it through. Ann and I found a way to survive, mostly through grit, hard work, determination, and, most certainly, the grace of God.

I remember an agent asking me "Teresa, do you remember the moment in the crash when you realized that you had no idea when the bottom would hit?" I knew just what she meant. As we started the downward descent of values I kept thinking "it can't go any lower". And the next week that repeated until a moment in time when you realized that you had absolutely no idea how far the market could fall. That was the moment of reality that you were in a free fall that you couldn't predict and couldn't possibly control. It felt like sky diving without a parachute.

I've heard it said that "what doesn't kill you makes you stronger". Harsh winters produce beautiful flowers in the spring. I can attest that the difficult time spent in the real estate crash made me better......stronger, more knowledgeable, more resilient, more compassionate. Not that I'd ever want to experience it again, mind you. Once through the fire is enough for me. Still, it did refine us.

Today as we write this book, the real estate market in our area has bounced back to near where it was before the crash. Let's hope we never again experience a market shift even remotely as severe as what we experienced in Florida from 2007 to 2010. But you never know what tomorrow will bring. Real estate is a market. Not as volatile as the stock market, but a market nonetheless. Sometimes it goes up, and sometimes it goes down.

Buying smart, whether in a great market or a depressed market, is so important. And a Real Estate Professional can help you buy smart. Does that mean you'd never lose on your purchase? Of course not. But if you buy smart you will be less likely to lose big and more likely to regain sooner when the inevitable rebound comes.

As a Real Estate Agent developing your business model and budget, it is so important to budget for savings, and also to consider ways to achieve multiple streams of income that will be valuable to you in the event the real estate market declines. Many Agents buy properties they can put into rental status to create another stream of income and build equity. Others invest in other businesses to provide for additional income to invest or save for those tough times in a market shift. When you think of getting your real estate license be thinking about all the various avenues you can pursue that will help to round out and balance your business income.

People tend to get into the real estate business when it is prosperous, and buyers and sellers abound. But beware of the "U" when you get in and prepare for it, because you most likely will encounter it at some point in your career. What goes up, can and likely will go down!

KENDALL'S KORNER.........THE BROKER VIEW

I have been a lawyer, at the time this book was written, over 15 years. During that time, my husband, also a lawyer, predicted that a crash was coming about 2.5 years before it happened. So what did he do? He started a Bankruptcy Law Firm in 2005! Imagine that! It was during the HEIGHT of the market and seemed like the thing least needed by consumers at that time. Needless to say, he was right. We filed bankruptcies for so many families, Realtors®, lenders, and homeowners during that time. We did our best to help customers get a fresh start. Many of those past clients are still our clients today. That law firm was a part of my path to where I am now. When I first entered the real estate industry it was during some of the hardest times to sell a home. We learned how to help, and so we did. Even now, we are still helping folks buy homes that were affected by that market crash over 10 years later.

The path and journey of home ownership is peppered with ups, downs, twists, and turns. Experience matters. Care matters. You matter.

SO THEN......YOU STILL WANT TO BE A REAL ESTATE AGENT?

Like any other profession, being a real estate agent has its challenges, but it also provides one with the opportunity to create and develop your own business with a limited investment and an unlimited opportunity. It allows you to work in a community of fun, resourceful, hard-working, and caring professionals. It provides a tremendous opportunity to help people in making one of the most important and life defining decisions of their life.........their home. It is a stressful decision that you can help make less stressful. It is a complex financial transaction that you can help people navigate successfully.

Getting started in real estate isn't necessarily easy. Each state has its own requirements for licensing and laws about what you can and cannot do. We recommend you do your research for your particular area.

There is ongoing training absolutely needed in order to do the job........everything from filling out a contract, financing rules and process, techniques for market analysis, tips on working with buyers, how to conduct a listing appointment.....the education needed is extensive and will continue throughout your career. The first lessons in real estate are to learn what your legal requirements are to get licensed, the type of license your state requires, and how to affiliate with a local brokerage, a local board of Realtors®, and a local multiple listing service.

You'll find a wide variety of personalities in most real estate brokerages, but the common thread is that most real estate people have an entrepreneurial, enthusiastic spirit. The field doesn't tend to attract people who like everything the same every day. It attracts people who are excited by new challenges and varied work days, and people who interact well with others. That makes most brokerages fun work environments. No matter your age, gender, nationality, or ethnic background you are welcome and can thrive in a real estate career. They sky is the limit if you are willing to learn, work hard, and help people. Limits are only the ones you put on yourself.

But perhaps the most rewarding part of the business is knowing that your expertise really helps people. Recently, I ran into buyers I helped buy a house a number of years ago. When they purchased the house they had two very young little boys. Now those boys are teenagers. Their Mom introduced me as "the lady that helped us find our house". She told me how happy they had been in their home and the community and I felt like I got paid all over again. It is priceless when that happens, and it happens a lot. You can make a difference in people's lives that last for years to come and provide them a life of memories. How many professions can say that? As Real Estate Professionals, we are proud of the value we provide.

KENDALL'S KORNER.........THE BROKER VIEW

To be or not to be… that is the question. If after reading this book, you still want to pursue a career in real estate – I'm not surprised! You are reading the words of two wise and dedicated Realtors®

However, the truth of the matter is this – most people that attempt this business QUIT. Why do they quit so often, so easily, so predictably? Oh so many reason. But what I'd rather tell you is how NOT to fall into that trap! Do your research, talk to others in the business, set aside a budget to fund your investment. Remember you are investing in an opportunity. You will need to make wise decisions about where you affiliate, the training you receive (not all trainers are created equal), and the expenses you will pay.

The most important problem I see as a Broker is that people fail to take action! They know what they should do, and yet they don't do it. I could tell you how important a goal and a plan are, but will you take the time to create, write, and maintain one? I can tell you how important a coach and mentor are, but will you invest in one? I can tell you how to master your skills and improve them, but will you do what it takes to grow? Most people say "Yes!" and DO nothing.... That is why so many quit! It's not fear of rejection, or lack of experience or that they don't have any leads. Those are the excuses they tell themselves to avoid the lesson in failure. Will you ignore this lesson or take vital action?

What will YOU DO?

BLOWN AWAY

On a Friday in the early part of November I had visited one of my listings to deliver some new flyers and check on the house. I had a little extra time, so I decided before heading home to stop at a strip mall to buy a birthday present for my assistant whose birthday was coming up. I parked in the parking lot, but it looked like it was about to rain so I decided to just leave the mall, head home, and shop for her on the weekend. As I started out of the parking lot headed to the major road way, I received a tornado alert on my phone. Suddenly it was looking quite dark in the sky. I turned on the radio in my car and heard a very dire, very insistent tornado warning alert. It said a tornado warning was in effect and to take cover immediately. I made the decision not to go out on the main roadway, but to return to the parking lot where I had just been. I parked the car in the strip mall parking lot and planned to wait in the car. The alert on the radio was becoming frightening and the sky looked dark and weird. The rain started coming down hard. The alert said to take cover in a substantial building. I debated with myself whether to stay in the car alone and risk the car being picked up, or to try to make a run in the rain for one of the stores while I thought I could. I made the decision to run for the building. I was almost to the door of the store when the wind pushed hard against me, then picked me up and threw me in front of the next store. I came down hard and knew immediately that my leg was broken. I was also bleeding but wasn't sure where I was cut. The wind was whirling around and I could barely see. I knew the tornado was upon me. An amazing, courageous lady, an angel to be sure, came out of one of the stores, helped me get inside the building, and called 911.

I ended up being taken by ambulance to the closest trauma center hospital. I had a forehead laceration, a broken left hand, a broken right toe.........and a badly broken left leg. The leg required two surgeries. I spent 6 days in the hospital, 6 days in a rehab center, and could not put weight on my left leg for 3 months........no walking, no driving. At the end of the 3 months I had to learn to walk again.

When life throws you a curve it is surprising how kind, caring, and giving people can be, especially the real estate community. So many of my fellow Agents came to visit me or sent cards, flowers, gifts, and offered their assistance to help with anything I might need. Especially Ann Carlson. Thank you, Ann, for all you did for me. Realtors® are a caring bunch of people.....and I experienced that first hand when I needed it most.

KENDALL'S KORNER.........THE BROKER VIEW

I remember where I was and what I was doing when Teresa called me to tell me what happened to her. To say I was in shock would be an understatement. Our office and Agents were devastated for her. Teresa is a prepared person and didn't really need our help because she literally had it all under control mentally and financially within days of this crazy event. As you can imagine, I am often humbled and honored while working with Teresa and Ann. Through this experience, Teresa was able to lean on her friend and colleague, Ann, who faithfully volunteered as her personal "taxi" driver and sales business partner, all the while maintaining her own hectic and successful business.

Teresa and Ann are right – the people you will meet in our industry are potential friends, family, and neighbors.

The lesson I think you should learn from Teresa's experience that day is this: entrepreneurs and business owners are financially vulnerable. Although Teresa was prepared, I find most Agents are not. When you lose your W-2 status and gain a 1099, you also lose employer paid benefits like health insurance, disability insurance, retirement plans, dental, vision, and life insurance. However, it doesn't mean that you don't need these things. In fact, maybe more so! If you are reading this right now and you are a Real Estate Professional – don't neglect these things. I know they seem expensive, but how much more would it cost you if something happened and you didn't have those resources. They are important and could provide the assistance you need when you need it. No one could have predicted a tornado would pick Teresa up, toss her and she would survive – but it happened. Life happens. Be prepared.